HIDE & SPEAK
ITALIAN

Catherine Bruzzone and Susan Martineau
Italian text: Catherine Bruzzone and Maria Adelaide Binns
Illustrated by Louise Comfort

b small publishing

Alla fattoria – On the farm

1	**Il gatto** corre dietro al topo.	1	**The cat** is chasing **the mouse**.
2	**Il cane** dorme al sole.	2	**The dog** is sleeping in the sun.
3	**Il cavallo** è nella stalla.	3	**The horse** is in the stable.
4	**La mucca** dà il latte.	4	**The cow** gives milk.
5	**Il maiale** mangia molto!	5	**The pig** is eating a lot!
6	**Le pecore** sono nel prato.	6	**The sheep** are in the field.
7	**L'anatra** nuota nello stagno.	7	**The duck** is swimming on the pond.
8	**La capra** mangia l'erba.	8	**The goat** is eating grass.

il gatto

eel gat-to

il topo

eel toh-po

il cane

eel cah-neh

il cavallo

eel kah-val-lo

la mucca

lah moo-ka

il maiale

eel my-ah-leh

la pecora

lah peh-kora

l'anatra

lah-nah-tra

la capra

lah kah-pra

Nella classe - In the classroom

1	**La maestra** dice "Silenzio!"	1	**The teacher** calls "Silence!"
2	Barbara è **sulla sedia**.	2	Barbara is on **the chair**.
3	Pietro è sotto **il tavolo**.	3	Peter is under **the table**.
4	Matteo tira **il libro**.	4	Matthew is throwing **the book**.
5	Isabella scarabocchia con **le matite colorate**.	5	Isabel is scribbling with **the coloured pencils**.
6	Roberto lascia cadere **la colla**.	6	Robert drops **the glue**.
7	Maria taglia **la carta**.	7	Mary is cutting up **the paper**.
8	**La penna** è **sul tavolo**.	8	**The pen** is on **the table**.
9	E Paolo gioca tranquillamente con **il computer**!	9	And Paul is playing quietly with **the computer**!

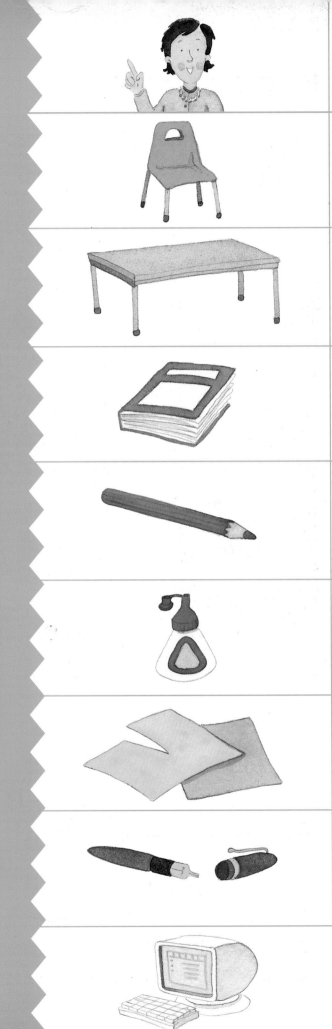

la maestra

lah mah-aistra

la sedia

lah sed-ya

il tavolo

eel tah-volo

il libro

eel leebro

la matita colorata

lah matee-ta kolorah-ta

la colla

lah kol-la

la carta

lah kar-ta

la penna

lah pen-na

il computer

eel compew-tair

Toccati la testa - Touch your head

1	Mi tocco **la testa**.	1	I'm touching **my head**.
2	Mi tocco **gli occhi**.	2	I'm touching **my eyes**.
3	Mi tocco **il naso**.	3	I'm touching **my nose**.
4	Mi tocco **la bocca**.	4	I'm touching **my mouth**.
5	Mi tocco **le spalle**.	5	I'm touching **my shoulders**.
6	Mi tocco **il braccio**.	6	I'm touching **my arm**.
7	Mi tocco **la mano**.	7	I'm touching **my hand**.
8	Mi tocco **la gamba**.	8	I'm touching **my leg**.
9	Mi tocco **il piede**.	9	I'm touching **my foot**.

la testa
lah teh-sta

gli occhi
l-yee oh-kee

il naso
eel nah-zo

la bocca
lah bok-ka

le spalle
leh spah-leh

il braccio
eel brah-cho

la mano
lah mah-no

la gamba
lah gam-ba

il piede
eel pee-yeh-deh

Nella giungla - In the jungle

1	una coccinella **rossa**		1	a **red** ladybird
2	una farfalla **blu**		2	a **blue** butterfly
3	una foglia **verde**		3	a **green** leaf
4	un frutto **giallo**		4	a **yellow** fruit
5	un pappagallo **arancione**		5	an **orange** parrot
6	una formica **nera**		6	a **black** ant
7	una farfalla **bianca**		7	a **white** butterfly
8	un fiore **viola**		8	a **purple** flower
9	un ramo **marrone**		9	a **brown** branch

rosso/rossa

ro-sso/ro-ssa

blu

bloo

verde

vairdeh

giallo/gialla

jal-lo/jal-la

arancione

aran-choh-neh

nero/nera

nair-o/nair-a

bianco/bianca

bee-anko/bee-anka

viola

veeo-la

marrone

mah-ro-neh

1	Mi metto **la gonna**.	1	I'm putting on **the skirt**.
2	Ti metti **il vestito**?	2	Are you putting on **the dress**?
3	Carolina si mette **i pantaloni**.	3	Caroline is putting on **the trousers**.
4	Giacomo si mette **il cappotto**.	4	James is putting on **the coat**.
5	Ci mettiamo **le scarpe**.	5	We're putting on **the shoes**.
6	Giovanni e Tommaso si mettono **la camicia**.	6	John and Thomas are putting on **the shirt**.
7	Lucia si mette **il pigiama**.	7	Lucy is putting on **the pyjamas**.
8	Il bebè si mette **i calzini**.	8	The baby is putting on **the socks**.
9	Il cane si mette **il cappello**.	9	The dog is putting on **the hat**.

I vestiti - Clothes

la gonna

lah gon-na

il vestito

eel vestee-to

i pantaloni

ee pantalo-nee

il cappotto

eel kap-pot-to

le scarpe

leh skar-peh

la camicia

lah kamee-cha

il pigiama

el peejah-ma

i calzini

ee kalt-zee-nee

il cappello

eel kap-pel-lo

Una giornata allo zoo - A day at the zoo

1	**La giraffa** ha un piccolino.	1	**The giraffe** has a baby.
2	**Il leone** dorme sotto un albero.	2	**The lion** is sleeping under the tree.
3	**La tigre** mangia il suo pasto.	3	**The tiger** is eating its meal.
4	**L'elefante** si lava.	4	**The elephant** is washing.
5	**Il coccodrillo** nuota nel lago.	5	**The crocodile** is swimming in the lake.
6	**Il serpente** è sull'albero.	6	**The snake** is in the tree.
7	**L'orso polare** s'arrampica su una roccia.	7	**The polar bear** is climbing on a rock.
8	**All'ippopotamo** piace il fango.	8	**The hippopotamus** likes mud.
9	**Il delfino** salta in aria.	9	**The dolphin** is jumping in the air.

la giraffa

lah jee-raf-a

il leone

eel layoh-neh

la tigre

lah teegreh

l'elefante

leleh-fanteh

il coccodrillo

eel kokkodreel-lo

il serpente

eel sairp-enteh

l'orso polare

lorso polar-eh

l'ippopotamo

leep-po-po-tah-mo

il delfino

eel delfeen-o

Nella strada - In the street

1 La signora attraversa **la strada**.

2 I bambini sono **sul marciapiede**.

3 **L'autobus** si ferma **alla fermata**.

4 **Il camion** si ferma **al semaforo**.

5 Il ragazzo è **sulla bicicletta**.

6 **La macchina** è rossa.

7 **La macchina della polizia** va veloce.

1 The woman is crossing **the street**.

2 The children are on **the pavement**.

3 **The bus** stops at **the bus stop**.

4 **The lorry** stops at **the traffic lights**.

5 The boy is on **the bicycle**.

6 **The car** is red.

7 **The police car** is going fast.

la strada

lah strah-da

il marciapiede

eel marchah-pee-yaideh

l'autobus

laowtoboos

la fermata

lah fairmah-ta

il camion

eel kam-yon

il semaforo

eel sem-ah-foro

la bicicletta

lah bee-chee-klet-ta

la macchina

lah makeen-a

la macchina della polizia

lah makeen-a del-la poleet-zee-ya

Alla spiaggia - At the beach

1	**Il mare** è blu.		1	**The sea** is blue.
2	**La sabbia** è gialla.		2	**The sand** is yellow.
3	**Il gabbiano** mangia **il pesce**.		3	**The seagull** is eating **the fish**.
4	**L'alga** è verde.		4	**The seaweed** is green.
5	**La conchiglia** è **sulla roccia**.		5	**The shell** is on **the rock**.
6	I bambini sono **nella barca a vela**.		6	The children are in **the sailing boat**.
7	Ci sono molte **onde** grandi.		7	There are lots of big **waves**.

il mare

eel mar-eh

la sabbia

lah sab-ya

il gabbiano

eel gab-yan-o

il pesce

eel pesh-eh

l'alga

lal-ga

la conchiglia

lah kon-keel-ya

la roccia

lah roch-a

la barca a vela

lah barka ah vail-a

l'onda

londa

La mia famiglia - My family

1	**Mia madre** è seduta a tavola.	1	**My mother** is sitting at the table.
2	**Mio padre** parla con **mio nonno**.	2	**My father** is talking to **my grandfather**.
3	**Mio fratello** gioca con il suo trenino.	3	**My brother** is playing with his train.
4	**Mia nonna** mangia gli spaghetti.	4	**My grandmother** is eating spaghetti.
5	**Mia zia** aiuta **mia sorella**.	5	**My aunt** is helping **my sister**.
6	**Mio zio** beve acqua.	6	**My uncle** is drinking some water.
7	**I miei cugini** guardano la televisione.	7	**My cousins** are watching television.

mia madre/mamma

mee-a madreh/mam-ma

mio padre/papà

mee-o padreh/papa

mia sorella

mee-a soh-rel-la

mio fratello

mee-o frat-el-lo

mia nonna

mee-a non-na

mio nonno

mee-o non-no

mia zia

mee-a tzee-ya

mio zio

mee-o tzee-yo

i miei cugini

ee mee-ay-ee koo-jeen-ee

Giorno di festa! - Party time!

1	Anna mangia **un panino**.	1 Anne is eating **a sandwich**.
2	Il bebè vuole **del cioccolato**.	2 The baby wants **some chocolate**.
3	**La torta** è sulla tavola.	3 **The cake** is on the table.
4	**Le patate fritte** sono calde.	4 **The chips** are hot!
5	**La pizza** è quasi finita.	5 **The pizza** is almost finished.
6	Enrico ha **un gelato**.	6 Henry has **an ice-cream**.
7	Vuoi **una Coca Cola** o **un succo d'arancia**?	7 Do you want **coke** or **orange juice**?
8	Preferisco **l'acqua**.	8 I prefer **water**.

il panino

eel pan-een-o

il cioccolato

eel chokko-lah-to

la torta

lah tort-a

le patate fritte

leh patah-teh freet-teh

la pizza

lah peet-za

il gelato

eel jel-lah-to

la Coca Cola

lah koka ko-la

il succo d'arancia

eel sook-o da-rancha

l'acqua

lakwa

Comprare giocattoli - Shopping for toys

1	L'orsetto è più grande del bambino.	1	The teddy is bigger than the boy.
2	Sara gioca con il robot.	2	Sarah is playing with the robot.
3	Oscar vuole comprare la palla.	3	Oscar wants to buy the ball.
4	Preferisci il puzzle o il gioco?	4	Do you prefer the puzzle or the game?
5	Il calcio-balilla è molto divertente!	5	Table football is really fun!
6	Cristina e Guglielmo guardano il videogioco.	6	Christina and William are looking at the computer game.
7	Il papà compra il modellino di aeroplano.	7	Dad is buying the model aeroplane.
8	Alle ragazze piacciono le perline.	8	The girls like the beads.

l'orsetto

lorset-to

il robot

eel rob-o

la palla

lah pal-la

il puzzle

eel poot-zleh

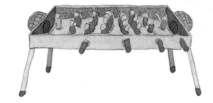

il gioco

eel jock-o

il calcio-balilla

eel kalcho balee-la

il videogioco

eel veed-ay-o-jock-o

il modellino di aeroplano

eel model-leen-o dee ah-air-o-plah-no

le perline

leh pair-leen-eh

23

Lavare i piatti - Washing up

1   Il papà lava i piatti **nel lavello**.

2   La mamma taglia la mela con **il coltello**.

3   **Il cucchiaio** e **la forchetta** sono sporchi.

4   Giulia ha **un bicchiere** d'acqua.

5   Il gatto guarda **nel frigo**!

6   **Il piatto** cade.

7   **Le pentole** sono **sul fornello**.

1   Daddy is washing up in **the sink**.

2   Mummy is cutting the apple with **the knife**.

3   **The spoon** and **the fork** are dirty.

4   Julia has **a glass** of water.

5   The cat is looking in **the fridge**!

6   **The plate** is falling down.

7   **The saucepans** are on **the cooker**.

	il lavello *eel la<u>vel</u>-lo*
	il coltello *eel kol-<u>tel</u>-o*
	il cucchiaio *eel kookee-<u>ah</u>-yo*
	la forchetta *lah for<u>ket</u>-a*
	il bicchiere *eel bik-ee-<u>air</u>-eh*
	il frigo *eel <u>free</u>go*
	il piatto *eel pee-<u>at</u>-to*
	la pentola *lah <u>pen</u>tola*
	il fornello *eel for-<u>nel</u>-o*

In campagna - In the country

1	Elena si arrampica **sull'albero**.	1	Helen is climbing **the tree**.
2	**L'erba** è verde.	2	**The grass** is green.
3	**Il campo** è pieno di **fiori**.	3	**The field** is full of **flowers**.
4	**La montagna** è molto alta.	4	**The mountain** is very high.
5	Ci sono molti **alberi nel bosco**.	5	There are a lot of **trees** in **the wood**.
6	**Il ponte** attraversa **il fiume**.	6	**The bridge** crosses the **river**.
7	**L'uccello** fa il suo nido.	7	**The bird** is making its nest.

l'albero

lal-bair-o

l'erba

lairbah

il campo

eel kamp-o

il fiore

eel fee-or-eh

la montagna

lah montan-ya

il bosco

eel bosko

il ponte

eel ponteh

il fiume

eel fee-oom-eh

l'uccello

loo-chel-o

Fare il bagno - Having a bath

1	Simone si lava con **il sapone**.	1	Simon is washing himself with **the soap**.
2	**Il lavandino** è pieno d'acqua.	2	**The washbasin** is full of water.
3	Luca gioca con **la doccia**.	3	Luke is playing with **the shower**.
4	Il gatto dorme **sull'asciugamano**.	4	The cat is sleeping on **the towel**.
5	**Il gabinetto** è accanto **alla vasca da bagno**.	5	**The toilet** is next to **the bath**.
6	Margherita mette **il dentifricio sullo spazzolino**.	6	Margaret is putting **toothpaste** on **the toothbrush.**
7	**Lo specchio** è sopra **il lavandino**.	7	**The mirror** is above **the washbasin**.

il sapone

eel sapo-neh

il lavandino

eel lavandee-no

la doccia

lah doh-cha

l'asciugamano

lashooga-ma-no

il gabinetto

eel gabeenet-to

la vasca da bagno

lah vaska dah banyo

il dentifricio

eel dentee-free-cho

lo spazzolino

lo spat-zoleeno

lo specchio

lo spek-yo

29

Nella mia camera - In my bedroom

1	Dormo nel **mio letto**.	1	I'm sleeping in **my bed**.
2	**La sveglia** è **sullo scaffale**.	2	**The alarm clock** is on **the shelf**.
3	Mi piace guardare **la televisione**.	3	I like watching **television**.
4	**Il mio letto** è vicino **alla finestra**.	4	**My bed** is near **the window**.
5	I miei vestiti sono **nell'armadio**.	5	My clothes are in **the wardrobe**.
6	**Il mio Walkman** è **sul tappeto**.	6	**My Walkman** is on **the rug**.
7	La mamma apre **la porta**.	7	Mummy is opening **the door**.